Psalms

"...Tumble into Springtime aburst with joy."

Psalms
For Life Living
by D.N. Sutton

Copyright © 1994 & 2000 by D.N. Sutton
All Rights Reserved
Cover By Ida Candelaria

ISBN: 0-940361-22-1
Printed in USA by Acorn Press

Sherwood-Spencer Publishing
The SoulSite Press: www.SoulSite.com
The SoulSite Shop: soulsite.com/shop
The SoulSite Library: soulsite.com/library
SoulSite Contact: sutton@soulsite.com

For Pam
*whose early inspiration and faithful heart
led to this moment*

Psalms

For Life Living

Springtime Comes	1
O People Be	2
Winter No More	3
Homecoming	4
New Era	5
I Am Your Brook	6
Who Will Speak Out?	7
God Aloft	8
Cousins Begin	9
The Music, I	10
One Harbor	11
Miracles	12
You Are God's Child	13
You As You Are	14
Aurora	15
Come, Inheritors	16
God Is The One Reality	17
The Total Cathedral	18
No More Resist	19
For Who Are We?	20
Love God With Wild Abandon	21
Child of Earth	22
In This Great Forgiving	23
Forgive	24
God Is No Fearful Giant	25
House of Life	26
Communion	27
In These Holy Hours	28
Until We Trust	29
So You Are Beyond God	30
And So The Lord God Comes Down	31
Hidden Code	32
In The Palm of Your Hand	33

Springtime Comes

O God
Springtime comes.

Out of your creation
Comes the sun, the green
The garden.

So long the waiting
So deep the longing
So limited the knowing...

O God
As the green wave breaks over your world
New insights cleansing old hates
May we baptise ourselves in your desires
Be agents of your Springtime.

May we be lifted to your breast
Filled to our brimming
Bringing ourselves into
The channels of your will.

O People Be

People,
Sir, Madame,
Boy, Girl, Child...

Are you nonentity, statistic, thing
Or do you have identity?
Are you no one, nothing
Or is God in you
Singing loudly in your veins?
Is faith in you
Stronger than bland logic
Sailing you out over the roof-tops of self-doubt
Swinging you into deep-being?

O People
Hear the inner melody
Grab on to the carousel of courage
Shout the dark down with your bright imaginings
Drink in deeply the energies of the universal
And know you are in God's design
You, uniquely you.

O People Be.
Call out to God in one another
Sense his fullness
Even in the smallness of all beings
And kicking the winter down
All together
Tumble into Springtime
Aburst with joy.

Winter No More

Spirit, take us!
We, who bathe in your essence
Feed at your core
May we
In this world
Move to your winds
Drink deeply of your well
Not only later
When the body leaves us
Free-falling in your splendor
But now in this life
In this flesh
That we may live in wonder at your closeness
That each breath sing your being
Each word shape your meaning
Each move strengthen us, fledgeling persons
Only now learning to fly
Into the dawn of your presence.

Like blind bats waking from the cave
Of our own darkness
We blink, trembling
At your unexpected light.

Spirit
May we be under your hand
Bringing in your Springtime
Winter no more.

Homecoming

Friend
Hear the Springtime singing in the self
God's love outpouring
Into you
The cup of your body
Holding his essence
He runneth over
In your veins.

Friend
Wanderer
All paths lead to one source
Look elsewhere no longer
For he is within
Waiting for your homecoming.

New Era

God of the Galaxies
Parent Universal
Leading us into your new era of commitment...
No more can narrow valleys of dogma
Contain the torrents of your commandments
Earthquakes of change
Catapult us from mean huts of habit
Into the palace of the encompassing Spirit.
We have outrun our old wisdom
Now newborn in fresh context of your closeness
Rich veins of your divinity deep within ourselves
Make your presence known within and without.

God of the Galaxies
Wiping away ancient hates with new awareness
Entrusting us with your Springtime
Transform us, bewildered Earth children,
Cousins all
Into loving instruments of your takeover.

I Am Your Brook

Spirit
In you
I know all
Though I understand little
I breathe
And am blessed
Think, and when I open my mouth
Your words are spoken
You move my pen to write
My steps to walk
When I fear
You quiet me
In you is all protection
All shield
I yield my will, my substance, my person...
You are my identity.

In your strength
I now walk into the world
I who am not brave
Speak out against wrong
For I am sheathed in your purpose
I who am not wise
Lead others to your wisdom
Blessing even those who hate
Condemning no one
Leading all into the arms of your requirement.

I am your brook
And I will run joyfully
To the rim of the oceans
That the hemispheres overflow
With the surge of your Springtime.

Who Will Speak Out?

Where are the words?
Where is the will?
Where are the acts of love?
Who will speak out for the only reality – God?
Who knows the practical path in him?
Who breathes his constant presence?
Who serves his new dimension?

Beloved friend
Where are you?
You are being called
Onto new paths
Where no one has yet walked
For the era of Springtime comes to the earth
And you are its seed.

God Aloft

God aloft
Is within
Cosmic
Personal.

God Is,
By faith
By fact
Scientific pathways
Revealing truths,
Reality
Mirroring
Deity.

Human mind
Denies
God's charity?
Yet sun and moon
In orbit
Rise and set
Gravity confirmed,
World defined.

Our bodies
Holding the holy water of life
Perform
Dimensions measurable
Precision remarkable
Magically
Spelled out
In the flesh
While impartially
The universal time clock
Ticks away.

God aloft
God within
God is I
God is they
God is all.

Cousins Begin

How can we give thanks for the aliveness of Life?
Thirsting and the waters flow
Hungering and the feast laid out
Need answered
Call for love fulfilled!

How express joy in completion
Other than to sing it out
To share abundance
With all beloveds of earth?
How can we stand still
While there are drums to beat
Wild rivers of change to ford?
How breathe
Without hosannahs?

Life is beautiful and so must be death.
God is!
God is!
Cousins begin to love
For are we not all caught in His one lively net?

The Music, I

I am a sounding board
I hear tidal waves of music
As in some vast cathedral
I am the organ swelling
In chords of magnitude
I could not conceive myself
I rise out of body shell
Into winged power
See sunlight slanting
Color too vivid for mosaic
And the stained glass of emotion
Quivering in largest light.

Why am I the vessel of such delight
That I taste fruits blessed and unforbidden
Experience truth with stunning clarity
As though veils are rent?

Why am I, O Spirit, lifted out of myself
Enchanted in a way no doing of mine
Can explain?
I sense the vastness of the cosmos
Stand at the great door in the wall
And I hear, see, feel, know your nearness
Thrilled, enthralled
Utterly thine!

One Harbor

You
Are your own island
A place
Where sun and sea have meaning.

Where nothing was,
You are.
Winds sweep in
Tides swirl
Sea-birds find you.

Living
You are a lighthouse
On the uncertain coast.
Being,
Others groping
Find passage.
Standing,
Seemingly alone,
You project
Strength
Beam warmth.

Unknowing, even to yourself,
You bring in the lost
To One Harbor.

Miracles

If you want miracles
Seize them to your heart...
Dreams live and burn
Until they are born of flesh.

You are not hollow
An empty soul
You are not trapped
Unless you trap yourself!

God bursts in you
His energy ignites.
God blazes in you
And the fires that he lights
will not go out.

Go on!
Illuminate the world
With the beauty of the spirit
You are God's child, his glory
And his hope...
You are his essence and you
Cannot fail.

The Kingdom comes in you
And in your life, you are a King.

You Are God's Child

You are God's child and nestle in his hand
You are his agent on the earth
Pour out your love and let the ego go
Wisdom is beyond the flesh
It is not in us to know.

Be the benediction, the blessing
Let the world shine where you have walked
Feeling the Spirit seize you in the quick
You will need no special wings beneath your feet
No map of where to go.

Live, breathe, bless, blend, forgive, fulfill
And burst forth like a candle flame into the air
Warm, alive and light.
Blessings—God's child
Go on out—into the night!

You As You Are

You sing on
Even if the voice is quiet
If it is within
It is heard.
You are known, sensed
Experienced
A small wind
Rippling the larger lake.

You, tiny
Are immense.
Your breath alters the mist
The pebble under your foot
Adds to the universe of dust
Whirling to meet cosmic need.

You, who have come from the Before
Are here in the Now, not by accident.
You, who will leave for the Beyond
Are on loan to the earth—
Alive, vibrant, needed, wanted
To lend your beauty
Give your insight
Bring your healing...
Open fisted fingers
Into the strong softnesses of love
Without condemning
With your own patient being.

You as you are
Sing on
Even though the voice is quiet.
God in you
Blesses all.

Aurora

No one is an amoeba
Locked in a one-celled life
A speck of dirt on the lens of the universe.

No!

By the hand of God
A person is a many-faceted being
A jewel
Whose cuts and angles
Splendor the light
Whose colors are the spectrum.

No human is one thing
But is of the total range
In us all life dances
In us all life breathes.
No one is no thing
But all things
No one is zero
But God's splendor
No one is minus
For what we think we lack at this moment
Will come in a flood of abundance
And we will be fulfilled.

No one is more than any other
No one is less.
A person is a multiple miracle
An individual kaleidescope of lively lights
Reborn each minute in God's fresh aurora.

Come, Inheritors

Regal humans, us
Born on earth
To live thousandfold
The one exalted life—
Born again and again
By our own act of willingness
Merging joyfully into the One Will.

For are we not all cousins of the same blood
All lambs of the One Shepherd?
None are to be sacrificed to the lusts of the other
All have divine value
All are to live nobly
None are to perish.

Come, inheritors
Into your own kingdom on earth
Each human royal, hardworking, loving
Self-disciplined in the princely calling
Of servitude to God's cause.

God Is The One Reality

God is the one reality
God is life.
The joy in the life that God has given
Bursts one's mind.
God's love sweeps away all myth
Human structures are illusions
Thoughts circular
Institutions, time-bound
And with time crumble.
Only God is real.
Only God is permanent.
Only God is Life.

God Is.
He breathes his breath
Giving individual identity
A mirror of him for others.
Keeping your mirror clean
His light reflects clearly
So that by knowing you
We are made whole
Become more holy
For we who are born of the Spirit
Are the Spirit
And we who hear his call
Answer to it.
There is no kiss
Like the matchless kiss of God
And no life
That is not a joyous love-affair with him.

God is the one reality,
The only discipline.
In Him
We are.

Total Cathedral

Who is there greater than God
The maker of all matter
The giver of life to all living
Is any part ever more than the whole?

Magnificent manifestations of God
Are fractions of his allness
His messengers, saints
Prophets thundering evidence
Give glimpses of the vastnesses of his truth.

There is no end to his word or his universe
Only the beginning of his offering to man
For he flows in torrents of love and change
Revealing himself in the laws of reality.

God is beyond our mind and machinations
Beyond man-made devils, notions, potions
God cannot be trapped in myth or magic
Nor understood by human logic.

God is the house of life, the total cathedral
At which human intellect can only marvel.

No More Resist

Two thousand years
And still the crown of thorns
Presses into his head.
His sad eyes look on us,
Unbelieving
At our persisting unbelief.

We, using his name
Pierce his side
We, following his path
Mock him
Nailing him endlessly to the cross
Denying ourselves, as we deny him.

He, who gave his life
That we may live
Still we turn on him,
Cursing his roots
Hurting his family
The family of man.

Blind humans, us
When will love seize us,
Clear our eyes
Hold back our hand?
When will we free him,
Free ourselves?
This man loves,
Let no doubt confuse us.
This man lives,
Is, waits
Calls us now to humanness.
Who identifies with him
That in his agony
The agony of man
The brambles and blood
Be not in vain?

Two thousand years—
But now, no more resist
The Oneness of the Spirit.
The Jew, Jesus waits,
Love outpouring
For the human race
To claim its Christ.

For Who Are We?

Enough of hate!
The world has had its fill
Of basic dishonesty
Of blood vengeance.

We have bowed down to dogmas
Decimated truth to please human masters
Have been used cruelly and have cruelly used
Denied identity
Trampled on blessings given
Made little children to suffer
Women to grieve.

No more enslavement by our evil spirit!
Blind faith
Is like blind blame
Evokes heresy
Because it is heresy.
True faith is true love
And bears no yoke only that from God...
Each soul a sword drawn
That no human suffer wantonly
Nor be less than God-given
Each one priceless
In his image
Divinely made
Fulfilled divinely.

Enough of hate
For who are we
To be thieves of our own joy?

Love God With Wild Abandon

Love God with wild abandon
Fling self-pity to the winds
Embrace destiny with joy
Praise, for music and dance are prayer
Love, for all persons are of God
Forgive, for all are human in his sight.

Plan, for life must not drift
Work, for work is salvation
Do good and there will be less evil
Honor body and mind, for they are one.

Let the limit of being rest in the Spirit
No need to bear the burden of the universe!
In the name of the Creator be a creator
In the name of the Lord be his child.

Child Of Earth

Child of earth
Love God
With rock-like faith
With awesome, total, infinite giving of self
Life's love affair is a love affair with him
You, who are born of him and will return to him
Know your source and find your path.

Taste of him, drink of him, breathe of him
Lose yourself in him
Immerse yourself in his vastnesses
And you will fulfil and be fulfilled
You will be saved and will save
You will be his instrument and his messenger
You will be his and will exceed yourself
Beyond all boundaries.

For the glories of your genius are his mirror...
So human child
So rich in God, so full of God
Climb out of the cradle of the night
Into adulthood and the light.

In This Great Forgiving

Forgive, human creature
As forgives the Father.

Forgive your fellows, self, friend, cousin, brother
Forgive all ever done
Forgive all never done
Forgive all sin
Transgression, thoughtlessness or pain
All you have coveted, lost, loved or sought
Forgive all cruelty and bless all men
Knowing no suffering is lived in vain
Embrace the world for it is yours to love.

In this great forgiving
Is God's greatest gift
Life, Living.

Forgive

The self cries out – am I forgiven?
Forgive, human being, forgive
For we are all in error
All frail, lost, limited.

Even when the heart is honest
The hand kind
Even with God's impulse in the mind
We fail.
We fail ourselves, and one another.

Even with vast love and strong intention
Fate's intervention can
Bring us to our knees
It is not always slated that we please.
We cannot always claim a star...
Our failures are our blessings
Our hurts will find their healing balms
If we give each other alms.

In order that we all may live
Forgive, human being, forgive.

God Is No Fearful Giant

God is no fearful giant in the sky
Nor are you Jack-on-the-beanstalk
Wavering and quavering on a tipsy vine...
Thinking you'll beat him in some comic duel
Of words or incantation, deal or threat
Is cosmic silliness!

Climb down from fanciful uncertainties
Face God in yourself
You are your own giant
Fill your boots with the divine force
Find within yourself the source.

Life's too vast for explaining or complaining
Worms do not interpret Scripture, for all their toil
They work and keep still and that done
Enrich the soil.

House of Life

God, timeless tower of all strength
No one speaks with your mighty lips
No one stands in your awesome shoes
No one is empowered with your authority.

The before and the hereafter are your mystery
All gifts are from you, all pacts with you
Almighty parent, hold us close
We know there is no living without you
We sense, in our limited wisdom
That hatred is insult to the spirit
That bigots cast themselves out of the realms of joy
Into their own consuming fires.

God, calling to us in this fateful hour
Taking us, each one, into everloving arms
Lead us into your shining House of Life.

Communion

Come celebrate the festival of our lives
Fiesta of living
Beauty spilled at our feet
Joy splashed on our being.

Come celebrate the feast of commitment
Dance of participation
Singing of communion
Foot on the path.

Come sample the flesh of holiness
Blood of love
Repatriate the self
In the arms of God.

In These Holy Hours

In these holy hours
Are we not his annointed
His children
His loves
His special persons
Transmitters of his seed
Purveyor of his thoughts
Continuators of his human race?

Now we must face ourselves
Our pure calling
Our main purpose
And all the exultation and
Excitement of aliveness.

In these holy hours
In this holy cause
Bringing together
Hating tribes of earth
Into loving oneness
In these holy hours
Kingdom prophesied
Kingdom Come!

Until We Trust

Believing is only beginning
Until we trust.
The word God
And the word of God
Are meaningless
Empty mouthings
Unless, unless
The soul quivers in the nearness
Is of the Isness, in
Affirmation beyond word or words.

Believing is only beginning
Until we trust.
What counts, what counts
Is our spiritual nakedness
Our intense vulnerability
In the power of the Presence
Mind-blowing love
That takes no contradiction...
Blessed release of fear.

The word, the words
Come only as close as we come
As close as we are
Believing is only beginning
Until we trust.

So You Are Beyond God

So you are beyond God
A human
Immune to the longings
Of the other side of the self.
If you have
Total perception
Can encompass
All experience
In your own entity,
Be utterly island
Even in currents
Beyond control
Then you are indeed splendid.

You are aware enough
To be sickened
By wrongs done
In the name of right
So choose
Some mid-ground
Where brain offers a small cup
To the parched spirit,
Some small sip of other wine.

You who believe you are beyond God
Are seeking to be beyond man.
Intelligent being
Put it all together
Now that you have broken it down
So neatly,
Discover Him.

And So The Lord God Comes Down

And so the Lord God comes down
From behind His islands of the planets
Flooding our beings with words
Till eyes weep with tears
The awe of it, the clarity of it
A clear arc across the skies
Of our limited understanding.

The pen writes
While the heart fills
With ineffable love, peace and purpose,
The Lord God of the Universe
In every bit of flesh
Drift of mind.

And so the Lord God comes down
Savage cells stilled at last
In clear vision of our godliness.

Hidden Code

O God
We live in your shadow
Spilling love freely
From the bottomless cup
Of thanksgiving.

The life given us
Empty, but for you
Brims over.
We ask little
Have all.
Offer a few grains
And are given golden loaves.
Share
And are blessed
Beyond contribution.

How do miracles occur
In this age of practicality?
Romanticism is out-of-date
Alchemy, unscientific
Dogma unfeeling
But love
The breath of the living God
Links strangers
Warms chill
Makes clear one denominator.

So, friend
Thank him, as we give
His love, the hidden code by which
To live.

In The Palm Of Your Hand

In the palm of your hand
Oh Lord
In the palm of your hand
You hold us.

In your calm
We quiet
In your love
We heal.

No more a stranger
To your touch
No more alone
Your benediction
Quells fear
Dispels doubt
Brings into clarity
Infinity.

Hold us
Oh Lord
In the palm of your hand
The palm of your hand.